Culinary BOND
A FATHER-DAUGHTER COOKBOOK

KEAUNDRA PRICE WITH CHEF LARRY PRICE

Culinary Bond
A FATHER-DAUGHTER COOKBOOK

KEAUNDRA PRICE WITH CHEF LARRY PRICE

Copyright © 2024 by Keaundra Price

All rights reserved.

No portion of this book may be reproduced in any form without written permission from the publisher or author, except as permitted by U.S. copyright law.

This publication is designed to provide accurate and authoritative information in regard to the subject matter covered. It is sold with the understanding that neither the author nor the publisher is engaged in rendering legal, investment, accounting or other professional services. While the publisher and author have used their best efforts in preparing this book, they make no representations or warranties with respect to the accuracy or completeness of the contents of this book and specifically disclaim any implied warranties of merchantability or fitness for a particular purpose. No warranty may be created or extended by sales representatives or written sales materials. The advice and strategies contained herein may not be suitable for your situation. You should consult with a professional when appropriate. Neither the publisher nor the author shall be liable for any loss of profit or any other commercial damages, including but not limited to special, incidental, consequential, personal, or other damages.

Photography by Marcus D. Porter Studios

First Ed. 2024

Hardbook ISBN: 979-8-218-44594-2

Ebook ISBN: 979-8-218-45026-7

This book is dedicated to my father, a true culinary artist and the greatest cook I have ever known.

Dad, your passion for cooking and your unwavering dedication to excellence have profoundly shaped my life. Through your hard work, dedication, and tireless pursuit of perfection in the kitchen, you have inspired me to embrace my own love for cooking.

From you, I have learned that cooking is not just about following recipes, but about expressing creativity, and care for others. Your influence is the heartbeat of this cookbook, blending your cherished recipes with my own culinary experiments.

Who knew that I, the non-chef, would grow up to write a cookbook? It's funny how life pans out—here I am, putting this project together and collaborating with you, the professional. You deserve all the recognition in the world for your talent and dedication. You are, in my eyes, one of the greatest chefs to ever grace the kitchen.

This book is a testament to your legacy and the invaluable lessons you have imparted to me. Thank you for being my mentor, my inspiration, and the best cook in the world. This is for you, Dad.

CONTENTS

- **INTRODUCTION** 11
- **MAIN DISHES** 20
  - Italian Casserole 21
  - Classic Burger 22
  - Chuck Roast Tacos 23
  - Beef Stroganoff 24
  - Shrimp and Grits 25
  - Creamy Tuscan Garlic Chicken 27
  - Poulet Saute 28
- **STARTERS** 30
  - Stuffed Peppers 31
  - Fried Green Tomatoes 32
  - Turkey Meatballs 33
- **SIDES** 34
  - Italian Spinach 35
  - Southern Fried Corn 36
  - Southern Fried Cabbage 37
- **DESSERT** 38
  - Key Lime Pie 39
  - Bananaless Pudding (No Bake) 41
  - Apple Dumpling 43
  - Red Velvet Cake 44
  - Blondie 46
  - 1-Layer Oreo Cake 47
  - Sweet Potato Pie 48
  - French Apple Pie 49
- **SOUPS** 50
  - Chicken Pot Pie Soup 51
  - Potato Soup 54
- **BREAKFAST AND BREADS** 56
  - Biscuits 57
  - Lemon Blueberry Muffins 58
  - Hot Water Cornbread 60
- **MEET CHEF LARRY AND KEAUNDRA** 63
- **ACKNOWLEDGMENTS** 70

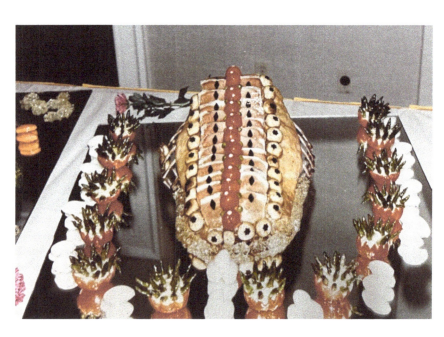

INTRODUCTION

Since I was a little girl, I've loved my daddy's cooking. Some of my earliest memories are of my dad competing for chef tastings, while my brother and I served as his miniature sous chefs. From our home to locations all over the world, I had the privilege of seeing my dad shine as an award-winning personal and executive chef, serving clients like President George Bush, Dixie Carter, David Gest, Anfernee Hardaway, and a host of other politicians, professional athletes, actors and entertainers.

I absorbed many qualities from him as I grew up — good character, integrity, hard work, and more. Yet, my favorite take away from my father was his love for cooking. In the kitchen, my dad wasn't just a teacher but a mentor, guiding me through the intricacies of food preparation with patience and precision. From the proper way to wield a knife to the balance of flavors that define a perfect dish, his lessons were infused with a sense of tradition and a commitment to excellence.

It was my father's encouragement to trust my instincts that empowered me to embrace the art of cooking with a sense of freedom and expression. This encouragement led me to build on his early lessons and pursue culinary courses at Harvard. Now, I'm no chef, but I proudly walk in my father's legacy, which is marked by a love for the art of cooking and the science of baking. It's a legacy I am honored to share with you all.

I've always believed that cooking, for my father, was much more than a talent but a God-given gift shared generously with others. It is my hope that creating this cookbook in his honor will return the gift to him and allow him to feel some of the love he's given me.

While I could fill the pages of this book with memories and inspiration from my dad, I'd like to share some words from friends he's gained on his culinary journey:

"I first met Larry through a mutual friend on a nice summer day in 1996. I was on a mission to find a top personal chef and I felt as though God sent me Larry. I didn't know that our first meeting would become a 28-year journey of service and it's still going.

Larry Price is the best chef in the world. He's cared for my family and I in more areas than the kitchen, and he's become family to me."

-Anfernee "Penny" Hardaway
former NBA all-Star

"I first met Chef Larry Price back in the early '90s at an American Culinary Federation Memphis Chapter meeting. Chef Price was one of only a handful of young African American chefs in charge of a corporate high-end hotel during that period. I was struck by Chef Price's polished professional stature and the confidence and respect he commanded when you were in his presence.

The next time I saw Chef Price was not in person but in a Commercial Appeal newspaper article highlighting his skill and talent as Executive Chef for Holiday Inn at Brooks Road. That article inspired me to set my goals high and become an Executive Chef, just like Chef Price.

Many years have passed since then. Chef Price and I are both very accomplished African American chefs in the greater Memphis area, but most importantly, we are best friends and more like brothers. Larry Price remains a role model and mentor for many generations of black chefs who came after him. My brotherly love for Larry Price is unshakable and permanently fixed in my heart."

-Chef Steven Leake
Southwest Tennessee Community College & Owner of Premier Ice Sculpture

"I first met Larry over 30 years ago when we both worked at the Memphis Hunt & Polo Club. He became more than a colleague—he was a mentor. Larry's skills and precise

approach to cooking inspired me. I often sought his advice on recipes, techniques, & presentation. His guidance played a significant role in shaping my culinary career.

Beyond our professional relationship, Larry's friendship and support have been constant sources of inspiration. I am fortunate to have had such an amazing mentor and friend."

-Chef Carolyn Bailey
Memphis Hunt & Polo Club

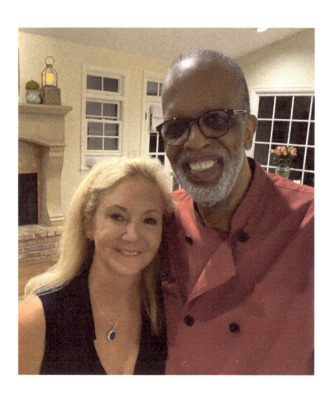

"In the realm of culinary artistry, few can craft not just meals but moments. Chef Larry stands out as a maestro of flavors, a mentor, and a beacon of excellence.

Working with him at River Terrace Yacht Club and teaching at the Penal Farm, his presence was more than that of a chef; it was a promise of perfection and magic in every dish. His leadership and passion were unwavering, dedicated to his colleagues, students, and craft.

As a colleague, he embodied teamwork and generosity, always willing to share his knowledge. His humility, despite immense talent, showed that true greatness lies in the impact on others. He has truly impacted my life.

Beyond the kitchen, he is a friend, confidant, and has been a source of unwavering support for 25 years. In happy moments, for example when I was named Chef of the year, or when I married my husband, Scott, Larry was the first to raise a toast.

Reflecting on countless shared memories, his legacy endures. His culinary creations will continue to delight, his wisdom will guide aspiring chefs, and his spirit will inspire all who know him. Most importantly, I'm proud to call him my friend."

-Chef Valerie Bearup
Morris Marketing Group

Discover a culinary journey that spans generations. In this cookbook, I share treasured recipes with my father, a seasoned Executive Chef, whose passion for cooking has shaped my own. From family favorites to innovative creations, each dish tells a story of tradition and culinary expression.

MAIN DISHES

ITALIAN CASSEROLE

RECIPE BY Keaundra

SERVES 4-6

INGREDIENTS

1 ½ lbs beef

1 tsp seasoned salt

¼ tsp pepper

½ tsp garlic powder

¼ tsp minced garlic

¼ tsp italian seasoning

16 oz tomato sauce

1 tbsp tomato paste

1 tsp McCormick spaghetti seasoning mix (optional)

8 oz sour cream

8 oz Mexican cheese blend

8 oz crescent rolls (Pillsbury original)

DIRECTIONS

In a large skillet, add beef and seasonings. Cook until the beef is completely done. Drain any excess grease.

On low heat, add minced garlic, spaghetti seasoning mix, tomato sauce and tomato paste. Simmer for 5 to 10 minutes. Add additional seasoning to taste.

Add beef to a medium baking dish.

In a bowl, mix together sour cream and cheese. Spread cheese mixture over the top of the beef.

Without separating, spread the crescent roll sheet on top of the cheese mixture.

In a 400 degree oven, bake for 20 to 30 minutes or until golden brown.

Cool for 15 minutes and serve.

CLASSIC BURGER

RECIPE BY   Chef Larry

SERVES   4

INGREDIENTS

1 lb ground beef

1 large egg

1 tsp onion powder

1 tsp garlic powder

1 tsp Worcestershire sauce

1 ½ tbsp tomato sauce

1 tsp seasoned salt

1 tsp pepper

DIRECTIONS

Mix all ingredients together in a mixing bowl.

Incorporate completely by using your hands, squeezing the mixture to work it all in. Shape beef into 4 patties.

In a skillet on medium-high heat, cook patties for 4 to 5 minutes on each side (medium well) or until desired doneness. Remove from heat and serve.

CHUCK ROAST TACOS

RECIPE BY Keaundra

SERVES 4

INGREDIENTS

ROAST

2 lbs boneless ground chuck

Salt (to preference)

Pepper (to preference)

2 tbsp taco seasoning

GUACAMOLE

4 large avocados

Juice of 1 lime

2 - 3 tbsp red onion, finely chopped

¼ fresh cilantro chopped

Salt to taste

Pepper to taste

Garlic powder taste

Onion powder to taste

DIRECTIONS

Preheat the oven to 325 degrees. Season roast generously on both sides with salt, pepper and taco seasoning. Add to a baking dish and cover. Bake for 2 and a half hours. Depending on the size and cut of the roast, baking time may increase.

Remove roast from oven and shred using two forks. If the roast does not pull easily, add back into the oven for another 30 minutes.

Toss shredded roast in the rendered fat. At this point, if you would like more crispy ends, add back in the oven uncovered for 20 minutes.

NOTE
For every pound of chuck roast, bake for 1 hour and 15 minutes.

BEEF STROGANOFF

RECIPE BY Chef Larry

SERVES 4

INGREDIENTS

1 ½ lbs beef tenderloin (pound out)

1 tbsp vegetable oil

1 large onion, sliced

10 oz mushroom

3 tbsp butter

2 tbsp flour

2 cups beef broth

1 tbsp Dijon mustard

⅔ cup sour cream

Salt (to preference)

Pepper (to preference)

DIRECTIONS

Pound out beef, then slice into thin strips. Sprinkle it with salt and pepper.

Heat the skillet over high and cook beef on both sides until done. Remove from the skillet.

Reduce heat to medium and melt butter in skillet

Add onions and mushrooms. Cook until mushrooms are golden brown.

Add flour and scrape pan. Cook while stirring for 1 minute. Slowly whisk and add broth.

Add sour cream and mustard. Simmer.

Reduce heat to medium low for 3 to 5 minutes. Add salt and pepper to taste.

Add beef back to the sauce and simmer for 3 to 5 minutes, then remove from the stove.

Serve over rice or pasta.

NOTE
Serve over rice or pasta

SHRIMP AND GRITS

RECIPE BY Keaundra

SERVES 4

INGREDIENTS

GRITS

2 cups water

2 ½ cups chicken broth

1 tsp salt

1 cup stone-ground grits

2 cups shredded cheddar cheese (optional)

3 tbsp butter

SHRIMP

5 slices bacon, chopped

1 bell pepper, chopped

1 lb shrimp, peeled and deveined

1 tsp cajun seasoning

3 green onions chopped

3 garlic cloves, minced

¼ tsp salt

¾ cup chicken broth

1 tbsp lemon juice

2 tbsp chopped parsley

DIRECTIONS

GRITS

In a medium pot, bring broth, water and salt to a boil. Slowly whisk in grits. Reduce the heat to low and simmer, stirring often for 20 to 25 minutes until the grits are cooked.

Remove from heat and stir in cheese and butter until melted. Cover and keep warm.

SHRIMP

In a large skillet, cook bacon until crispy. Remove and drain on paper towels.

Add bell pepper to bacon drippings and saute over medium heat until tender.

Add shrimp, green onions, cajun seasoning, garlic and salt. Cook for 2 minutes (1 minute on each side). Stir in chicken broth and simmer for 5 minutes.

Right before serving, stir in the cooked bacon and lemon juice. Spoon the shrimp mixture over the grits and garnish with parsley, if desired.

CREAMY TUSCAN GARLIC CHICKEN

RECIPE BY Chef Larry

SERVES 4

INGREDIENTS

1 ½ lbs boneless skinless chicken breasts, thinly sliced

2 tbsp olive oil

1 cup heavy cream

½ cup chicken broth

1 tsp garlic powder

1 tsp Italian seasoning

½ cup parmesan cheese

½ cup spinach, chopped

½ cup sun-dried tomatoes

Salt (to preference)

Pepper (to preference)

DIRECTIONS

Season chicken to your liking. In a large skillet, add olive oil and cook chicken on medium high heat for 3-5 minutes on each side or until brown on each side and completely cooked. Remove chicken and set aside.

In the same skillet, add heavy cream, chicken broth, garlic powder, Italian seasoning and parmesan cheese. Whisk over medium high heat until the mixture begins to thicken.

Add spinach and sundried tomatoes. Simmer until spinach starts to wilt.

Add chicken back to the pan, add salt and pepper to taste.

Serve over pasta if desired.

NOTE
If you are serving over pasta and prefer it saucy, double the sauce.

POULET SAUTE

RECIPE BY Chef Larry

SERVES 4

INGREDIENTS

4 bone-in chicken breast (with skin)

4 ounces vegetable oil

1 cup all-purpose flour

Salt (to preference)

Pepper (to preference)

½ stick of butter (cubed)

1 cup chicken broth

½ yellow onion (sliced)

DIRECTIONS

In a frying skillet or dutch oven, heat vegetable oil over medium high heat.

Season chicken with salt and pepper. Coat chicken in flour.

Place chicken breasts in the skillet with the skin down first. Cook until golden brown (1 ½ to 2 minutes). Flip chicken breasts over and cook until golden brown.

Add chicken breasts to a baking dish along with butter, chicken broth, and onions and cover with foil.

In a 350 degree oven, bake for 1 hour.

NOTE
After 30 minutes of baking, baste the chicken with the broth mixture.

STARTERS

STUFFED PEPPERS

RECIPE BY Keaundra

SERVES 10

INGREDIENTS

1 lb mild Italian sausage

8 ounces cream cheese, cubed

1 tbsp onion powder

30 fresh sweet mini peppers (halved lengthwise and deseeded)

¼ cup parmesan cheese

DIRECTIONS

Preheat the oven to 350 degrees. Lightly grease a baking sheet with nonstick spray and set aside.

Add sausage to a skillet over medium heat. Cook sausage until brown and fully cooked through; drain excess grease. Reduce heat to low.

Add cream cheese to sausage and cook until cheese is fully melted and evenly mixed together. Add onion powder. Remove from heat.

Spoon sausage-cheese mixture into pepper halves and arrange on a prepared baking sheet. Sprinkle the parmesan cheese over stuffed peppers.

Bake for 30 minutes or until peppers are soft and cheese is golden brown.

NOTE
When stuffing the peppers, it's easier to use your hands with cooking gloves.

FRIED GREEN TOMATOES

RECIPE BY   Chef Larry

SERVES   4

INGREDIENTS

1 large green tomato

1 cup buttermilk

1 egg

½ cup cornmeal

½ cup bread crumbs

1 tsp kosher salt

½ tsp pepper

¼ tsp cayenne pepper

1 cup vegetable oil

DIRECTIONS

Cut tomato into four slices (⅜ in.).

Heat vegetable oil in a medium skillet on medium heat.

Mix milk and egg in a bowl and set aside. In a separate bowl, mix together cornmeal, bread crumbs, salt, pepper and cayenne pepper.

Add flour to a plate. Dip tomatoes in flour, followed by buttermilk mixture and then the cornmeal mixture last (fully coated)

Fry on both side until golden brown.

TURKEY MEATBALLS

RECIPE BY Chef Larry

SERVES 4-6 (should make 12 meatballs)

INGREDIENTS

1 lb ground turkey

1 tbsp dijon mustard

1 tbsp Worcestershire sauce

1 tsp garlic powder

1 tsp onion powder

1 large egg, lightly beaten

Pepper (to preference)

Salt (to preference)

1 egg

Nonstick cooking spray

DIRECTIONS

In a medium bowl, combine ground turkey, mustard, Worcestershire sauce, garlic powder, onion powder and egg.

Shape mixture into 2 ½ inch meatball patties. Season lightly with salt and pepper.

Lightly grease a griddle or skillet and heat over medium-high heat.

Cook meatball patties until done, 2 to 3 minutes on each side. Remove from heat.

SIDES

ITALIAN SPINACH

RECIPE BY Chef Larry

SERVES 3-4

INGREDIENTS

10 ounces of spinach (stems removed)

2 ounces extra virgin olive oil

2 tsp butter

Salt (to preference)

Pepper (to preference)

1 tbsp minced garlic

2 tbsp parmesan (freshly grated)

DIRECTIONS

Place olive oil in a saute or fry pan over medium heat then add butter.

Add spinach and continue to cook over medium heat, turning the spinach constantly with tongs.

When the spinach has wilted, add garlic, then salt and pepper to taste. Toss and incorporate thoroughly.

Mix in parmesan and serve.

SOUTHERN FRIED CORN

RECIPE BY Keaundra

SERVES 4-6

INGREDIENTS

6 ears of corn, shucked

3 slices of bacon, chopped

4 tbsp butter

1 tbsp sugar

¼ heavy cream

½ stick of butter

½ red bell pepper, chopped

½ green bell pepper, chopped

1 tsp salt

1 tsp pepper

DIRECTIONS

In a large skillet, cook chopped bacon until crispy and set aside.

Reduce heat to medium and add butter to the skillet with the bacon drippings.

Once the butter has melted add corn to the skillet and stir.

Add chopped bell peppers, salt, and pepper and simmer covered for 10 minutes.

Add heavy cream and sugar. Cover and simmer for 10 to 15 minutes on low heat.

Stir and add additional salt, pepper and sugar to desired taste.

SOUTHERN FRIED CABBAGE

RECIPE BY Keaundra

SERVES 4-6

INGREDIENTS

1 head of lettuce, roughly chopped

1 onion, roughly chopped

1 green bell pepper, chopped

5 strips of bacon, chopped

½ lb kielbasa sausage, chopped

2 tbsp butter

1 clove garlic, minced

Salt (to preference)

Pepper (to preference)

DIRECTIONS

Remove core and roughly chop lettuce; set aside.

In a large skillet, add butter and cook bacon until crispy. Remove bacon from the skillet and set aside. Leave bacon drippings and butter in the skillet.

On medium heat, add onions and bell pepper to the skillet and cook for 3 to 5 minutes.

Add sausage to the skillet and cook for 2 minutes. Add bacon back to the skillet and add garlic.

Add lettuce to the skillet, stir and cover for 5 to 10 minutes, stirring occasionally.

Add salt and pepper to taste.

Cook cabbage until desired texture. Remove from heat.

DESSERT

KEY LIME PIE

RECIPE BY Keaundra

SERVES 4-6

INGREDIENTS

4 tbsp unsalted butter, melted

8.8 oz (1 pkg) Biscoff cookies

21 oz (1 ½ cans) sweetened condensed milk

⅔ cup fresh key lime juice (roughly 8 key limes or limes)

3 egg yolks

2 tsp lime zest (zest of 2-3 key limes)

1 tsp vanilla extract

FOR DECORATION

1 cup heavy cream

3 tbsp powdered sugar

1 tsp vanilla

DIRECTIONS

Heat oven to 350 degrees.

Add cookies to a food processor and pulse until you have fine crumbs. Drizzle in the melted butter and pulse until combined. Note: If you don't have a processor, use a plastic bag and rolling pin to finely crumble, then just mix the crumbs and butter in a large bowl.

Evenly distribute the mixture into a 9" pie dish. Use a flat-bottomed glass or measuring cup to press the crumbs down firmly. You can use your fingers to press the top down as the side Is compressed.

Bake the crust at 350 degrees for 10 minutes.

While the crust Is baking, zest two limes and set aside. Squeeze roughly 8 limes for ⅔ cup of juice, straining out the seeds.

Add the egg yolks and zest to the bowl. Use a mixer to whisk for one minute.

Pour in the sweetened condensed milk and mix on medium until fully incorporated. Scrape the bowl down.

On low speed, pour in the key lime juice. Scrape the bowl down once more and mix.

Pour the filling into the warm crust and give it a jiggle to level things out. Bake at 350 degrees for 10 minutes.

Cool on a wire rack for 20 minutes and chill for at least an hour.

Top the pie with dollops of whipped cream and serve.

NOTE
When making the whipped cream, make sure to use a chilled bowl and mixer.

BANANALESS PUDDING (NO BAKE)

RECIPE BY Keaundra

SERVES 8-10

INGREDIENTS

3.4 oz Banana Cream (Jell-O brand preferred)

3 cups heavy cream

1 ½ cups cold water

14 oz sweetened condensed milk

1 tsp banana extract

½ tsp vanilla extract

1 box Nilla wafers cookies

Salted caramel (optional)

DIRECTIONS

PUDDING

In a medium bowl, whisk together banana cream pudding mix and cold water. Whisk in condensed milk until completely combined and smooth.

Cover and refrigerate for at least 4 hours or overnight to allow the pudding to become firm.

WHIPPED CREAM

In a large mixing bowl, add 3 cups of heavy cream, banana extract, and vanilla extract and whisk for 2-3 minutes using a mixer on high speed. The cream should turn into a fluffy "whipped cream." Do not over-whip.

Once the cream has turned into a whipped consistency, gently fold in the pudding mixture with a baking spatula or spoon. Do not over-whip or stir. Once all of the pudding is added, mix on low to ensure pudding and whipped cream are thoroughly combined.

In a serving dish, begin with a layer of the pudding/cream mixture, add cookies on top and repeat until the top and last layer are Nilla cookies.

Drizzle salted caramel on top and refrigerate for 3 to 4 hours before serving.

NOTE
When making the whipped cream, make sure to use a chilled bowl and mixer.

APPLE DUMPLING

RECIPE BY Keaundra

SERVES 12-16

INGREDIENTS

4 Granny Smith apples

2 pkg (8 oz each) crescent rolls (makes 16)

1 ½ cup orange juice

1 cup sugar

1 stick unsalted butter

½ tsp vanilla extract

½ tsp Nutmeg

DIRECTIONS

Heat oven to 350 degrees.

In a saucepan on low heat, heat the orange juice, sugar and butter until the butter is completely melted. Add vanilla and remove from heat.

Cut apples into fourths, discarding the core.

Open packages of crescent rolls and separate into individual pieces. Roll each apple into a crescent roll and add it to a baking dish.

Pour sauce mixture over dumplings.

Sprinkle a dash of nutmeg over each crescent. Bake for 15 to 20 minutes or until dumplings are golden brown. Cool for 15 minutes after baking.

NOTE
When rolling each dumpling, cover the apple as much as the dough will allow. Apples will soften while baking. If after 20 minutes the apples are not soft enough, continue to bake for 5 minutes. To prevent the top of the dumplings from browning too quickly, place a sheet of aluminum foil on top (do not seal the edges).

RED VELVET CAKE

RECIPE BY   Keaundra

SERVES   10-12

INGREDIENTS

2 ½ cups self-rising flour

1 cup buttermilk

1 ½ cups vegetable oil

1 tsp baking soda

1 tsp vanilla extract

1 oz red food coloring

1 ½ cups granulated sugar

1 tsp unsweetened cocoa powder

1 tsp white vinegar

2 large eggs

FOR FROSTING

⅓ lb (1 ⅓ sticks) butter, softened

10 oz cream cheese, softened

16 oz (1 lb) confectioners' sugar

2 cups chopped pecans (optional)

DIRECTIONS

Heat oven to 350 degrees. Spray three 9-inch round cake pans with nonstick coating.

Mix all dry ingredients together in one bowl, then all wet ingredients together in a separate bowl.

Combine wet ingredients with dry ingredients.

Pour batter equally into the three pans and bake for 20 minutes.

Test doneness with a toothpick. Cool layers in pans on wire racks for 10 minutes. Carefully remove layers from pans to rack to cool completely.

Combine butter, cream cheese and confectioners'

sugar to a bowl. Beat until fluffy, then fold in 1 ½ cups of pecans (optional). Fill layers between cakes and frost cake when it is cool.

Decorate the top of the cake with the remaining ½ cup of pecans; refrigerate at least 1 hour before serving.

NOTE
Do not overmix the batter. This recipe can be used for a sheet cake (13 x 9 inch baking pan) as well instead of the three 9-inch rounds. Sheet cake baking time increases to 40 to 45 minutes depending upon the oven. Use the toothpick test to ensure the cake is done.

BLONDIE

RECIPE BY Keaundra

SERVES 16

INGREDIENTS

2 ½ cups all-purpose flour

1 tbsp cornstarch

1 tsp baking soda

⅔ cup granulated sugar

¾ cup unsalted butter

1 large egg, room temperature

Additional 1 large egg yolk, room temperature

1 tbsp vanilla extract

1 cup white chocolate chips

DIRECTIONS

Preheat the oven to 350 degrees. Line a 9×9-inch baking pan with parchment paper.

In a medium mixing bowl, whisk together flour, cornstarch, baking soda, and salt.

In a separate large mixing bowl, add the brown sugar, granulated sugar, melted butter, egg, egg yolk, and vanilla. Whisk together until the mixture has thickened and fully combined.

Add the dry mixture to the wet mixture and stir together with a spatula until almost combined. Add the white chocolate chips and stir until they are well distributed.

Add dough to the baking pan and spread into an even layer.

Bake for about 35 minutes or until the edges are set and golden brown. Let the blondies cool completely in the pan before cutting.

NOTE

Use high-quality vanilla extract as this recipe relies a lot on the vanilla flavor. To ensure blondies are done, stick a toothpick towards the center of the blondie. It should come out clean with minimal (if any) crumbs.

1-LAYER OREO CAKE

RECIPE BY Keaundra

SERVES 8-10

INGREDIENTS

1 ¼ cups of all-purpose flour

1 ½ tsp baking powder

½ tsp salt

⅓ cup vegetable oil

⅔ cups granulated sugar

2 large eggs

½ cup milk

2 tsp vanilla

4 Oreo cookies (crushed)

FOR FROSTING

2 cups powdered sugar

4 tbsp melted butter

2 tsp vanilla extract

3 tsp milk

4 Oreo cookies (crushed)

DIRECTIONS

Heat oven to 350 degrees. Spray 9-inch round cake pan with nonstick coating.

In a medium bowl, which together oil, milk, eggs, sugar and vanilla extract.

In a separate bow, mix flour, baking powder and salt together.

Combine the wet and dry mixtures with a hand mixer or whisk until the batter is smooth.

Crush Oreos in a plastic bag or a food processor, then fold the crushed cookies into the batter.

Bake for 25 to 30 minutes.

SWEET POTATO PIE

RECIPE BY Chef Larry

SERVES 6-8

INGREDIENTS

3 large sweet potatoes

1 stick of butter, melted

¾ cup light brown sugar

½ cup sugar

2 large eggs, beaten

½ cup half & half

¾ tsp cinnamon

1 tsp nutmeg

9-inch pie shell

DIRECTIONS

Boil sweet potatoes for 30 minutes or until tender.

Mash sweet potatoes with a potato masher, then add butter.

Mix egg, half & half, sugars, cinnamon, and nutmeg in a separate bowl. Once combined, add to sweet potatoes.

Mix together all ingredients until smooth

Add mixture to pie shell and bake for up to 45 to 50 minutes in a 350 degree oven.

NOTE
Mash potatoes well to avoid any potato strings. Baking time will depend upon your oven. Check the pie after 30 minutes of baking.

FRENCH APPLE PIE

RECIPE BY Chef Larry

SERVES 6-8

INGREDIENTS

FILLING

6 cups Granny Smith apples, peeled and sliced

1 cup sugar

½ cup all-purpose flour

1 tsp vanilla extract

1 tsp salt (kosher)

2 cups sour cream

9-inch pie shell

TOPPING

1 ½ cups pecans

½ cup flour

¼ cup dark brown sugar

¼ cup sugar

5 ounces butter, unsalted and softened

1 tsp ground cinnamon

DIRECTIONS

Preheat the oven to 350 degrees.

Place apples in an unbaked pie shell.

Combine and mix all other filling ingredients.

Pour mixture over apples.

For the topping, grind pecans in a food processor. In a separate bowl, cream pecans, flour, sugars, butter and cinnamon together. Cover pie with the topping mixture.

Bake for 55 minutes.

SOUPS

CHICKEN POT PIE SOUP

RECIPE BY Keaundra

SERVES 6-8

INGREDIENTS

3 cups cooked, shredded chicken

6 tbsp unsalted butter

3 medium carrots, peeled and chopped

3 celery stalks, chopped

1 medium yellow onion, diced

1 ½ cups mushrooms, sliced or chopped

5 garlic cloves, minced

1 tsp Cajun seasoning

⅓ cup all-purpose flour

6 cups chicken stock

1 lb yukon gold potatoes (peeled and cut into cubes)

2 tsp dress thyme

1 cup frozen corn

1 cup frozen peas

½ heavy cream

¼ cup chopped parsley

Salt (to preference)

Pepper (to preference)

DIRECTIONS

In a large pot, add butter over medium heat. Once the butter is melted, add onions, carrots, and celery. Cook and stir occasionally for 5 minutes, or until the vegetables are tender. Add mushrooms and fully cook (about 3 minutes).

Add garlic and Cajun seasoning. Add flour. Stir until it is fully incorporated and turns into a paste consistency (roux). Slowly add in the chicken stock and stir.

Add the potatoes, thyme, salt, and pepper.

Over medium-high heat, bring the mixture to a boil. Lower the heat and cook, stirring frequently, until the potatoes are fork tender for about 20 minutes. Soup should thicken.

Add in the chicken, corn, peas and heavy cream. Bring the soup back to a boil over medium heat. Simmer for 2 minutes, stir in the parsley, and serve.

NOTE
Enjoy a "crust" by adding homemade biscuits on the top. See biscuit recipe.

POTATO SOUP

RECIPE BY Keaundra

SERVES 6-8

INGREDIENTS

1 ½ lbs yukon gold potatoes, cleaned, peeled, and chopped

3 cups chicken stock

5 strips of thick cut bacon, chopped

¼ cup all-purpose flour

2 cups whole milk

½ cup heavy cream

1 yellow medium onion, diced

2 tbsp butter

1 tbsp minced garlic

1 tbsp low sodium chicken or vegetable base

16 oz Boursin cheese (garlic and herbs)

8 oz grated cheddar cheese

Salt (to preference)

Pepper (to preference)

Green onion (garnish)

DIRECTIONS

In a large pot, cook bacon until crispy. Remove and place on a paper towel. (Bacon is optional, but if you're using bacon, do not remove the bacon drippings from the pot.)

Add butter and diced onions to the pot and cook on medium heat until onions are tender (4-5 mins). Add garlic and chicken or vegetable base.

Add flour and stir. Once the mixture turns into a paste consistency (roux), add chicken stock, milk, and heavy cream. Bring to a simmer.

Bring mixture to a boil and add potatoes. Reduce heat; cover 15 to 20 minutes or until potatoes are fork tender. Stir occasionally to avoid sticking.

With a potato masher, roughly mash potatoes. Remove half of the potato chunks and set aside. With a hand or immersion blender, blend the remaining potato mixture in the pot.

Reduce to low heat. Add Boursin and cheddar cheese. Stir until melted.

Add remaining potato chunks back to the mixture and season with salt and pepper to taste. If desired, add bacon back to the mixture or use as a topping.

Serve topped with green onions, bacon and cheese.

NOTE
To control salt intake, use low sodium stock. Yukon gold potatoes are preferred because of their creamy consistency; however, any form of potato will work.

BREAKFAST AND BREADS

BISCUITS

SERVES 12

RECIPE BY Keaundra

INGREDIENTS

3 cups fine pastry flour or all-purpose flour

½ tsp baking soda

2 tbsp baking powder

1 tbsp sugar

1 ½ tsp kosher salt

14 tbsp unsalted butter, frozen

1 ¼ cups buttermilk

DIRECTIONS

Preheat the oven to 425 degrees. Whisk together the pastry flour, baking soda, baking powder, sugar, and salt in a large bowl. Grate the frozen butter over the flour mixture. Gently mix with your fingers until coarse.

Stir in the buttermilk until just combined. The dough will be slightly sticky.

Place the dough on a lightly floured surface and roll into a square that is 1 inch thick. Fold it in half twice to create a smaller square and gently roll the dough again into a square that is 1 inch thick. This will help create flaky layers. Using a 3 inch cookie cutter, cut out the biscuits by pressing down and pulling up. Don't twist; it will prevent the biscuit from rising.

Place biscuits in a parchment lined baking pan and place in the freezer for about 20 minutes. Brush the top of the biscuits with a little buttermilk and add flaky salt. Bake in the oven for 20 to 25 minutes, until the biscuits are golden brown. Brush with melted butter.

LEMON BLUEBERRY MUFFINS

RECIPE BY Keaundra

SERVES 12

INGREDIENTS

2 cups all-purpose flour

2 tsp baking powder

1 tsp salt (kosher)

8 oz fresh blueberries

¾ cup granulated sugar

½ cup unsalted butter, melted

2 large eggs (room temperature)

2 tsp vanilla extract

¾ cup whole milk (room temperature)

Coarse sugar for topping

DIRECTIONS

Preheat to 400 degrees. Line a 12-cup muffin pan with paper liners or use baking spray.

In a medium bowl, whisk together the flour, baking powder, and salt; set aside.

In a small bowl, combine the blueberries with a tablespoon of the dry mixture and toss to combine. This will help prevent them from sinking in the batter.

In a large mixing bowl, beat the sugar, butter, and eggs together on medium speed until light and fluffy, about 2 minutes. Beat in the vanilla.

Add the flour mixture into the butter mixture in 3 parts, alternating with half of the milk between flour additions.

Stir in the blueberries. Divide the batter among the paper liners. (They will be full.) Scatter more blueberries on top and sprinkle with coarse sugar, if desired.

Bake for 20 minutes or until the tops are golden brown and a toothpick inserted into the center comes out with a few moist crumbs. The muffins should cool in the tin for a few minutes before removing them and cooling on a wire rack.

HOT WATER CORNBREAD

SERVES 4

RECIPE BY Chef Larry

INGREDIENTS

1 cup ground cornmeal

½ tsp kosher salt

½ cup + 2-4 tbsp boiling water

2 tbsp unsalted butter

Canola oil

DIRECTIONS

In a bowl, whisk together cornmeal and salt.

Boil 1 cup of water. The water must be boiling in order to soften the cornmeal.

Stir in ½ cup boiling water to form a soft dough that holds its shape. Then, begin adding the remaining water 1 tablespoon at a time while stirring. Stir after each addition of water.

Stir in melted butter.

Let the dough rest for about 5-10 minutes.

In a cast iron skillet, heat 1/4 inch of canola oil.

When the oil is hot, shape the cornmeal mixture into ½ inch patties and place in the skillet.

Cook for 2-3 minutes on both sides or until golden brown. Remove from oil and place on a tray to drain.

MEET CHEF LARRY AND KEAUNDRA

CHEF LARRY

Larry Price, a native of Memphis, Tennessee, is an esteemed executive chef with over 45 years of culinary experience. His illustrious career has been marked by a passion for culinary excellence and a dedication to crafting unforgettable dining experiences. Larry has held positions such as Executive Chef at some of Memphis' most popular hotels, where he showcased his culinary prowess and innovative flair in the kitchen.

Throughout his career, Larry has had the privilege of serving as a personal chef to an array of notable clientele, including NBA athletes, actors, entertainers, and politicians. Notably, his enduring relationship with NBA All-Star Anfernee "Penny" Hardaway spans over 28 years, a testament to the trust and satisfaction his culinary creations evoke.

In addition to his culinary endeavors, Larry has been deeply involved in culinary education and community outreach. As a former educator at the Memphis Penal Farm, he shared his wealth of culinary knowledge and expertise, teaching culinary skills to inmates and providing them with valuable opportunities for personal growth and development.

Larry is also a proud member of the American Culinary Federation (ACF), an organization dedicated to promoting the culinary profession and advancing culinary excellence. Through the ACF, Chef Larry continues to stay abreast of the latest culinary trends and techniques, further enhancing his culinary repertoire and staying at the forefront of his field.

Renowned for his exceptional skills, creativity, and unwavering commitment to excellence, Larry is celebrated as a culinary visionary and mentor within the industry. His culinary creations continue to captivate and delight diners, leaving a lasting impression on all who have the pleasure of experiencing his culinary artistry. Chef Larry has also achieved recognition through winning numerous culinary competitions and chef tastings, further solidifying his status as a culinary icon.

KEAUNDRA

Keaundra Price, a native of Memphis, TN, graduated from the University of Memphis. After a successful marketing career in the pharmaceutical and healthcare industries, she transitioned to pursue her passion for counseling and mental health, obtaining a Master of Science in Addiction Counseling. Keaundra is the Founder and Executive Director of Camp Counsel, a nonprofit dedicated to supporting the mental and emotional health of children and teens.

Keaundra has extensive experience in both corporate America and ministry. With a comprehensive background, Keaundra's roles have spanned from project manager to executive director, chief of staff, executive pastor, and VP of operations. She is also the owner of CEO Consulting, a ministry consulting company focusing on developing community, experience, and operations within churches. CEO Consulting utilizes the psychology of people to enhance church systems, policies, and culture. With over ten years of leadership experience, she is passionate about organizational development and leadership. Currently, she is pursuing a Ph.D. in Counseling and Psychological Studies with a concentration in Industrial-Organizational.

Keaundra is dedicated to developing healthy organizations and helping individuals process their thoughts and feelings effectively. She also shares her insights and experiences as a YouTube content creator.

ACKNOWLEDGMENTS

This cookbook is a labor of love, and it wouldn't have been possible without the incredible support and contributions from many wonderful people.

First and foremost, I would like to express my deepest gratitude to my father, whose culinary expertise and passion inspired this project. His recipes and guidance have been invaluable, and this book is a testament to his lifelong dedication to the art of cooking.

Special thanks to Marcus Porter, whose exceptional photography brought our dishes to life, capturing the essence and beauty of each dish.

I am also grateful to Anfernee Hardaway, Chef Valerie Bearup, Chef Steven Leake, and Chef Carolyn Bailey for their valuable contributions to the book. Your input and support have been instrumental in making this cookbook a reality.

Thank you to my dear friend, Joya Matthews, for your insight, input, and encouragement. Your help in sorting through my ideas has been instrumental in bringing this book to life. I am deeply grateful for your support and friendship throughout this journey.

Lastly, a special thank you to my mother, Kemelyn, Price, without whom I could not have created this book. Your support and assistance in gathering information and photos made this book all the more special.

To everyone involved, your efforts, talent, and support have made this cookbook a reality. I am forever grateful. From the bottom of my heart, thank you.

Printed in the USA
CPSIA information can be obtained
at www.ICGtesting.com
JSHW070240040724
65790JS00001B/2